mac's year
1984

mac's year
1984

Cartoons from the Daily Mail

Stan McMurtry **mac**

SPHERE BOOKS LIMITED
London and Sydney

Produced in association with the Daily Mail

First published in Great Britain by Sphere Books Ltd 1984
30–32 Gray's Inn Road, London WC1X 8JL
Copyright © Stan McMurtry 1984
All cartoons are reproduced in this book by kind
permission of the Daily Mail

TRADE
MARK

Printed and bound in Great Britain by
Collins, Glasgow

'Oh that ? It's just a man, dear. We keep him for breeding purposes'

'We'll talk about the Pill later—have you got a tin opener?'

'Psst! Tell the lads to keep the noise down—we don't want to lose our day shift perks too'

'Don't just sit there! Help me get the place ready—Mummy's coming home!'

'The headache's still there, Dr Soames— maybe I could just have an aspirin?'

'Well, it's only midday here, Phil ol' sport—now, if you'll turf Randy
Andy out of his bunk for a reverse charge, person to person. . . .'

'Damned unfortunate after all that effort — he hasn't got a sex certificate to prove he's a man.'

'Right, Norman Get back down to British Leyland . . . Ivan—Plesseys . . . Bernard—Labour Party . . .'

'Frankly I'm always a little relieved when the school holidays are over.'

'I think I've been promoted—he's going to make me into a eunuch.'

THE EVOLUTION OF MAN

'THIS WAY, FOLKS.'

'It's amazing how all that aggression disappears when they're given the right environment.'

'Can't help feeling a bit guilty—Ron and Eileen guarding our place, while we're doin' over theirs'

'When you talk to the boys about cigarette smoking, headmaster, will you put in a word about whisky and wild, wild women?'

'Sorry sir. I've no idea where one could buy one's wife a peanut butter and anchovy sandwich at this time of night.'

'Gerald ! Have you been taking paper clips from the office again ?'

'. . . . and top of the charts for the sixth week running — Albert Figgins of Chelmsford'

'... and now, three cheers for the gallant losers ...'

'Nice, effortless lift, dear — we'll let you know.'

'I see Michael Foot has handed everything over, then.'

'By gum, lad—Geoff Boycott's angry'

'Galt ! Goo goes gere ? Gend or go ?'

'Don't sulk, Dr Richards—hand over the rejuve nation serum. We may need it as evidence.'

'Before we start, I'd like you all to meet one of the country's leading vasectomists, who will be passing amongst you ...'

BLACKPOOL ILLUMINATIONS, 1983

'Honestly! I've never even heard of Cecil Parkinson.'

'Before we remove the patient's tonsils, doctor, could we have a swift peek at your credentials?'

'HOW TRAGIC !'

'So much for the sexy stuff—have you anything for the larger woman?'

'. . . a Russian spokesman denounced the Grenada invasion as banditry and terrorism . . .'

'Watch for the telltale signs . . . What rubbish! I'd soon know if there was another woman.'

'Trust me . . . I light the blue touch paper and stand well back
— right back, 3,000 miles away in an underground shelter.'

'I don't mind punks stealing the ashtrays or sliding down
the bannisters—but when they get into the kennels . . .'

'Egon's certainly got them trying harder — here comes my boeuf bourguignon now'

'I'm sorry . . . unfortunately, Miss Vladivostok was the only one who knew the square root of 7,406,000,303½.'

'Nice to see that despite all her commitments in Kenya, the Queen has remembered Charles's birthday.'

'I expect your missus'll be giving up at Greenham and wanting to come home soon, eh Norman ?'

'He's sorry, but that nasty mouse is in his box again and it's going Squeak Squeak'

'I'm warning you Norman! Any more talk about a whole football
team ready for the 1998 season and I'm going home to mother!'

'Gee, Jackie was so trusting—some wives would've put a chastity belt on him'

'I don't care what they do on video—I only saw her in half !'

'It would've been a fine performance if it wasn't for the bodyguards'

'Must've changed his sign—he used to have a huge pair of spectacles hanging there'

'Damned shame—ruining a good career for a few bottles of Scotch.'

'Good news—Pettigrew should have the placards ready for our protest march by July 1986'

'. . . And when are you going to have a word with your son about getting drunk and stealing penguins?'

'So you thought the film was fairly realistic, Mr Heseltine ?'

'Me too. My wife keeps nipping off to Birmingham—frankly, I think it's a ghastly place.'

'Right, Mr Brown — if you'll just read, then sign the card . . .'

'. . . and with back pay, you owe me £76,362·05 !'

'Look, dear, I know it's in the script, but could you make your giant a teensy weensy bit more ferocious?'

'Has that irresponsible, disobedient, damned idiot, Botham arrived yet?'

'How many roubles would Mike Yarwood want for standing on a balcony in Moscow and waving at people?'

'Your New Year resolution could've waited till Mother had finished her bath . . .'

'Security's been tightened, ma'am—no more cheeky beggars will get in disguised as part of the royal household.'

'You should have seen the one that got away'

'Break it to me gently, Karen honey—which one's Mark Thatcher?'

'Be honest, Charles—you were secretly hoping some of the media would still try to follow us around.'

Havoc of the hurricane

'Remember the old days when they used to salute?'

'Dash it, old boy, I knew there was something different about
you since you pranged—you've shaved off your moustache.'

But now the paralysed soldier plans a civil ceremony

'. . . and if anyone knows any ridiculous, heartless cause or impediment why these two should not be lawfully joined together . . .'

'A little trick Boycott picked up on his travels — he hadn't the heart to have the committee thrown out of the club completely.'

Helicopters save 60 trapped in trains

4 DEAD IN BLIZZARD

That lady who said loving in the backs of cars could cause problems, certainly knew what she was talking about.'

'Not now, stupid !—I think we're being watched'

'Stop worrying — it was the Worshipful Company of Grocers who commissioned the thing after all . . .'

'Turn left at the Union Card Incinerator block, right at Body X-ray, through the Lie Detector building and Big Brother's office is third on the left.'

'I tell you, Omar, if business doesn't pick up soon, I'm tearing up his contract.'

'I wish I could get somebody to feel that sorry for me'

'That look velly nice spot, Tebbit sah—we'll build there.'

'It'll stop all the excuses, but can we get it to New Zealand by Friday?'

'Damned French baggage handlers ! The cases have burst open . . .'

'Ignore him, Bob , , , should've known the   Russkies would try to upstage us.'

'I do hope Dean isn't going to let the Test match ruin their chances.'

'Renata, dear—Watford's dirty kit has arrived.'

'Nip downstairs, Pettigrew, and check that lady's knickers.'

'Denis dear, I know you want to make Mark's girl feel at home, but you keep missing the spittoon.'

'Oh come, m'sieu — with your foot flat down, you should clear twenty lorries easily'

'You have to hand it to David Steel, he certainly knows how to get the publicity, eh Wedgie . . . ?'

'Think of your career, kid—just saunter up to Prince William and say "Hello gorgeous" '

'John—were you pushing someone from the clan MacGregor around on Tuesday?'

Murray's cold war on Maggie

By MICHAEL EDWARDS
Industrial Editor

TRAINS, buses and ferries could be badly hit tomorrow by TUC-backed strikes.

Leaders of the big unions lined up yesterday to promise support for lunchtime protest rallies called over the Government's ban on unions at the Cheltenham spy centre.

'What a pity, darling — by accepting the £1,000, you're going to miss Len Murray's day of action'

'What will the English send us next? First it was their lamb...'

'Go on, Ron, you were saying . . . about them being a load of namby-pamby old pansies . . .'

Tory backbench leader gives advice to Premier

'Jolly good idea of du Cann's — sharing the work load'

mac

The Mail rings round and finds it easy to get account details

'We've just spent our last 10p phoning your bank, guv, and they say you're good for a few quid.'

'Look Peter, look—it's the Ladybird sales rep.'

'... and lastly, have you got anything good for insomnia, indigestion or athlete's foot?'

Cricketers quizzed on cocaine and pot

'... and very soon he'll start off on that characteristically long run of his from behind the sightscreen...'

'Sorry—the hall's completely blocked with crates of booze and cigarettes'

'Mr Simpson — perhaps you've read about the Home Secretary's new idea . . . making law-breakers repair the damage they've done ?'

What a difference a romance makes

'Sorry to keep you . . . if Christina Onassis can lose 1½ stone before getting married, so can she.'

'Step on it, Gladys ! It's the police—you're probably driving too slowly'

'Hey Franco—da gentleman isa withholding payment of da bill until we start playing fair with Britain in da E.E.C.'

'It started off with "Bring your own nappies", then it was sheets, then . . .'

'What about it, son? They're looking for people to parachute behind the enemy lines and scare the hell out of them.'

'You're in luck lads—gentleman from a breakers yard found them blocking the road on his way to work this morning.'

'Forgive me, my child—but could I hear your confession later?'

New clashes feared as coalfield is split

'Another lot going to the Lancashire Flower Arranging Gala, sarge.'

SCARGILL'S WAR ON DEMOCRACY

'Has Comrade Scargill sent a map of how to get to this Nottingham place ?'

'Women ! The bailiffs warned them about the ro ad-widening scheme and they're still stubborn.'

Bailiffs rip heart out of Greenham protest

'I feel sorry for the Greenham women too, Wedgie dear, but . . .'

'He doesn't look like a Libyan to me either, but the British seemed very keen to deport him.'

'Ding-dong, Avon man calling—is your husband at home?'

'Remind me again—which of those is Scargill trying to bring down?'

'We didn't find any gelignite down the sewer, but what we did find we're sending back to Gaddafi'

'Oh. and Charles, about this kissing in public . . . not only was Edward terribly embarrassed, but . . .'

Controversy surrounds the birth of this famous sleepy four

'What more could I want? I have got everything I could ask for'
JANICE SMALE

Test-tube quads born

'I'm sorry but you don't have the right qualifications — you're married and childless'

'Having to wear a yashmak at the bank isn't so bad, but we're a bit disappointed with the company car.'

'I'm sorry, they're all busy right now . . . er, participating in the Long Jump'

'It makes you ashamed to be British, doesn't it?'

'Can you give us a description madam? Quite a few broke down on double yellow lines and had to be towed away.'

'So, no more plainclothes decoy duty in gay bars, I'm afraid, men—we've got to be in uniform.'

'Looks as if they're expecting another demo . . .'

'Nein, nein, der Liverpool Lullaby is not one of Herr   John's songs—are der any ozzer requests?'

'Dear Mum and Dad, well here I am at the Russian holiday camp . . . it's a bit like home really . . . .'

Two mothers to produce one child is pioneer doctors' plan

'No, no—I'm Mummy, this is Biological Mummy, this is Donor Daddy and that's Daddy.'

'I feel so proud ! To think we've just dined in the company of Viscount Althorp AND Tony Blackburn.'

'It's a jam manufacturer—want to know if they can use you as a symbol on the side of their jars . . .'

'Fascinating, Glenys — but we did hope you'd be doing "Guess the Weight of the Cake" again this year'

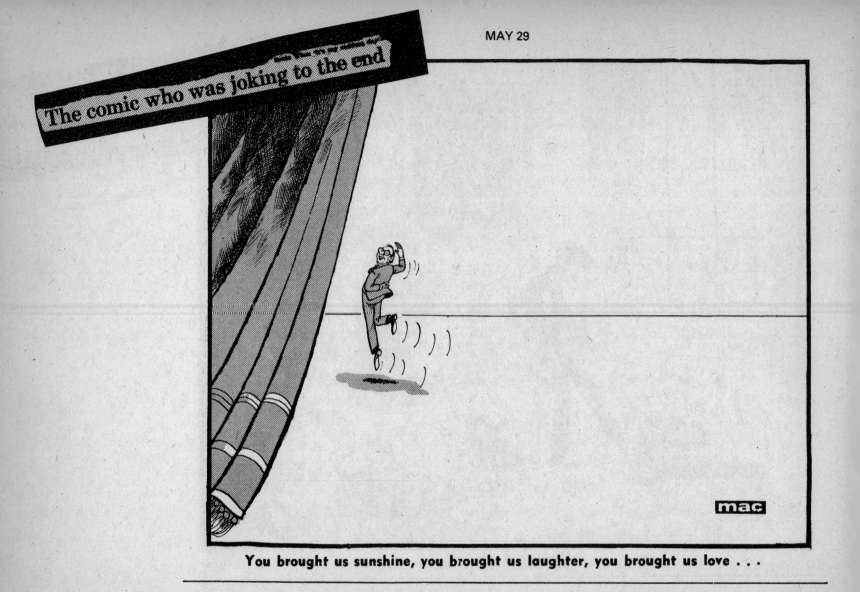

The comic who was joking to the end

You brought us sunshine, you brought us laughter, you brought us love . . .

'For heaven's sake, Charles! He's only a child!'

'Cecil, mon cher! 'Ave you come to re-enact what you did 40 years ago?'

'Bad news, Ron. Your cleaning lady just phoned—the White House has been burgled'

'Now then, Mr Podmore, about your application for a grant for an inside toilet . . .'